T0030937

TRAILBLAZING WOMEN IN
SOCCER

BY JOANNE MATTERN

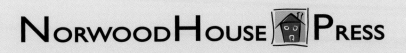

Cover: Crystal Dunn is one of the US Women's National Team's top defenders.

Norwood House Press

For information regarding Norwood House Press, please visit our website at:
www.norwoodhousepress.com or call 866-565-2900.

Credits
Editor: Katie Chanez and Patrick Donnelly
Designer: Becky Daum
Fact Checker: Lillian Dondero

PHOTO CREDITS: Cover: © Robin Alam/Icon Sportswire/AP Images; © Federico Guerra Moran/Shutterstock Images, 5; © Keith Johnston/Shutterstock Images, 7; © Al Messerschmidt/AP Images, 9; © Jeffrey A. Camarati/AP Images, 11; © Kevork Djansezian/AP Images, 15, 25; © Luca Bruno/AP Images, 17; © Bill Kostroun/AP Images, 19; © Yves Logghe/AP Images, 21; © Elise Amendola/AP Images, 23; © Martin Mejia/AP Images, 27; © Frank Augstein/AP Images, 28; © Paul Zoeller/AP Images, 31; © Petr David Josek/AP Images, 32; © Darryl Dyck/Jonathan Hayward/The Canadian Press/AP Images, 34; © Romain Biard/Shutterstock Images, 37, 41; © Gregory Bull/AP Images, 39; © Lev Radin/Shutterstock Images, 43; © Mikolaj Barbanell/Shutterstock Images, 45

Library of Congress Cataloging-in-Publication Data
Names: Mattern, Joanne, 1963- author.
Title: Trailblazing women in soccer / by Joanne Mattern.
Description: Chicago : Norwood House Press, 2023. | Series: Trailblazing female athletes | Includes bibliographical references and index. | Audience: Grades 4-6
Identifiers: LCCN 2022005089 (print) | LCCN 2022005090 (ebook) | ISBN 9781684507542 (hardcover) | ISBN 9781684048014 (paperback) | ISBN 9781684048076 (ebook)
Subjects: LCSH: Women soccer players--Biography--Juvenile literature.
Classification: LCC GV944.9.A1 M38 2023 (print) | LCC GV944.9.A1 (ebook) | DDC 796.334082--dc23/eng/20220209
LC record available at https://lccn.loc.gov/2022005089
LC ebook record available at https://lccn.loc.gov/2022005090

Hardcover ISBN: 978-1-68450-754-2
Paperback ISBN: 978-1-68404-801-4

353N—082022
Manufactured in the United States of America in North Mankato, Minnesota.

CONTENTS

WOMEN IN SOCCER

Soccer-like games have existed around the world for hundreds of years. The modern game was created in the mid-1800s in Great Britain. And from early on, women enjoyed playing the game just as men did. In fact, women's games sometimes attracted more fans than men's games did.

In Preston, England, factory workers created a team called Dick, Kerr Ladies. Fans flocked to stadiums to see the team and its star player, teenage winger Lily Parr. She could shoot the ball so hard she once broke a goalkeeper's arm. On Boxing Day in 1920, a crowd of 53,000 fans came out to watch a Dick, Kerr Ladies match in Liverpool.

The Football Association (FA) governs soccer in England. In 1921, it barred women from playing on official fields. This meant women

Soccer has gone from a pastime to a profession for many women.

had no place to play. The FA said that soccer was "unsuitable for females." That type of thinking about women's sports was common at the time. And England was not alone in banning women's soccer. Other countries effectively stopped women from playing through lack of support.

Those attitudes began to change during the 1970s. Bans were lifted. A new **federal** law called Title IX was enacted in the United States. Title IX wasn't created with sports in mind. However, its impact was perhaps best seen on the courts, fields, and rinks across the country. Schools that offered boys' sports teams now had to offer them for girls, too.

There were some attempts to establish women's soccer around that time. But the sport truly took off in the 1990s. By then, a generation of girls had grown up playing. FIFA, which governs global soccer, created the Women's World Cup in 1991. Women's soccer was added to the Olympics in 1996. Stars such as Mia Hamm and Sun Wen helped draw in fans. That showed in the huge crowds at the 1999 World Cup in the United States. Soon, superstars such as Megan Rapinoe of the United States and Brazil's Marta helped take the game to the next level with their skills and creativity. Now a new generation led by groundbreaking players such as Crystal Dunn is expanding the possibilities further.

In just a few decades, the Women's World Cup has grown into a major tournament. More than 1 billion people watched

Title IX helped create numerous opportunities for women in college athletics.

the 2019 event. Meanwhile, professional opportunities are booming, especially in the United States and Europe. The days of women being banned are distant memories in many parts of the world. However, there remains much work still to be done to provide equal opportunities for women.

CHAPTER ONE

MIA HAMM

The United States didn't have a women's national soccer team when Mariel Margaret Hamm was born. Even in schools, girls' sports teams were often underfunded—if they existed at all. Over her long soccer career, the woman who became known as Mia Hamm made sure nobody could overlook her sport ever again.

Hamm was born on March 17, 1972, in Selma, Alabama. Just a few months later, Title IX took effect. Hamm was from the first generation who grew up under those new rules.

Hamm's father was an Air Force pilot. The family moved a lot during her childhood. These moves brought Hamm closer to her brother. He was a

Mia Hamm was one of the first stars of the US Women's National Team.

soccer player. Before long, she was kicking a ball around too. It soon became clear that she was very good.

As more girls began playing sports, demand grew for higher-level competition. In the 1980s, a handful of countries began putting together women's national teams to compete with each other. The US Women's National Team (USWNT) was part of that movement. Hamm made her USWNT debut in 1987. At 15 years old, she was the team's youngest player. But she proved to be one of the team's best players before long.

QUICK FACT

Organizers weren't sure if they wanted to let women use the "World Cup" name. So the 1991 tournament was known at the time as the 1st FIFA World Championship for Women's Football for the M&M's Cup.

By 1991 the sport had grown enough to support a world championship tournament. It's now known as the Women's World Cup. Hamm was just 19 when she arrived in China for the event. She played in all six games for the US team and scored two goals. The hard-charging US team became the sport's first world champions.

Mia Hamm was a fan favorite and a role model for young players.

Leading the Revolution

The 1991 Women's World Cup had not been a major event. But it showed that athletes like Hamm were ready to compete on the world stage. Meanwhile, in the United States and elsewhere, more and more girls were playing sports. The 1996 Olympics were held in Atlanta, Georgia. For the first time, women's soccer and softball were included. It proved that people wanted to watch the top women compete. The United States and China met in the soccer final. More than 76,000 fans packed the stadium as Hamm and the US team won gold.

QUICK FACT

Hamm played college soccer at the University of North Carolina. The Tar Heels won the national title in each of Hamm's four seasons there.

Fans were eager to support the US team. Many were drawn particularly to Hamm. Quick and highly skilled, she was the team's best scorer. She wouldn't let anyone outwork her. Hamm showed that women could be superstar athletes too. And her popularity kept growing. Magazines wrote profile stories about her.

The Fab Five

Hamm emerged as one of the biggest stars in all of sports during the 1990s. She wasn't alone in pioneering women's soccer, though. She played much of her career alongside Julie Foudy, Joy Fawcett, Kristine Lilly, and Brandi Chastain. Fans nicknamed them the "Fab Five." Michelle Akers was another great US player of the era. She was the game's greatest scorer before Hamm arrived. By the end of her career in 2001, Akers had remade herself into a dominant defensive midfielder.

Companies paid big money for her to endorse their products. Most importantly, fans came out in big numbers to watch her play.

The 1999 Women's World Cup was set to take place in the United States. Organizers saw how popular Hamm and her teammates were becoming. They decided to take a risk. To host the games, they booked huge football stadiums. When the tournament began, that risk paid off. Huge crowds filled the stadiums. Many young fans—girls and boys— showed up in No. 9 Hamm jerseys. They were treated to a thrilling tournament. Hamm scored two goals and had two assists in the six US games.

The final brought an intense matchup between the United States and China. Neither team could score. That didn't stop Hamm from making an impact with her relentless effort. The US team ultimately won in a **shootout**. The final, held at the Rose Bowl in front of 90,185 fans, was the biggest women's sporting event ever. More than 40 million Americans watched on TV.

Hamm continued playing through 2004. In her final year she won a second Olympic gold medal. It went with two Women's World Cup titles. Hamm also retired as the sport's all-time leading scorer with 158 international goals. They were scored over her nearly two decades playing with the USWNT.

Yet her greatest impact might have come by example. Hamm knew people were watching. Though she didn't always love the attention, she embraced it. Even after her final game, she stayed to sign autographs. Her combination of ability and charisma helped introduce women's sports

From left, Mia Hamm, Kristine Lilly, and Brandi Chastain sing the national anthem after winning the gold-medal match at the 2004 Summer Olympics.

Hamm's goal-scoring record didn't last long. Fellow American Abby Wambach surpassed it in 2013. Then Canada's Christine Sinclair took it over when she scored her 185th goal in 2020.

to millions. Women's soccer has continued to grow since Hamm retired. Today it's a major sport around the world. Hamm and her peers in the 1990s showed what was possible.

Carli Lloyd

In 2003, Carli Lloyd was cut from the US Under-21 team. If she was going to make it as a player, she decided she had to do it her own way. Lloyd took up a famously aggressive training plan. She prided herself on outworking everyone else. Her intensity didn't always make her friends. But her results on the field were undeniable. Lloyd scored the gold-medal-winning goals at the 2008 and 2012 Olympics. She scored four goals in the 2015 Women's World Cup final. And in 2021, she retired on her own terms. Only one player in international soccer history had appeared in more than her 316 games. Just three had scored more than her 134 goals.

From left, Abby Wambach, Mia Hamm, Julie Foudy, and Kristine Lilly celebrate a goal against Brazil at the 2004 Olympics.

CHAPTER TWO

SUN WEN

Soccer is the one truly global team sport. Wherever people live, the game is played. As a result, different cultures approach the game in their own unique ways. So, while women's soccer was emerging in the United States and Europe, the sport began growing in China too.

Sun Wen was born on April 6, 1973, in Shanghai, China. China is the world's most populated country. However, for many years China chose not to take part in international sporting events like the Olympics. That began to change in the 1980s. To produce competitive athletes, China created sports schools. Promising young athletes could train and study there. When she was 13, Sun began attending one of these schools. Before long she had developed into a skilled soccer player.

Sun Wen (left) celebrates after scoring a goal against the United States.

With women's sports growing, China stepped up to host the first Women's World Cup in 1991. Sun, at age 18, proved to be one of China's key players. She started all four games as a midfielder. In a 2–2 draw against Denmark, she scored a goal. The tournament ended in disappointment for the hosts, as China lost in the quarterfinals. But China would soon emerge as a power in the sport, and Sun led the way.

Rising Sun

In the coming years Sun developed into a dangerous offensive player. She had a knack for scoring goals. She could shoot hard with either foot. However, if an opponent played her too close, Sun could burn her with a crafty pass. Sun led China to the semifinals at the 1995 Women's World Cup. One year later, women's soccer was an Olympic sport for the first time. This time Sun led her team to the final. However, they had to settle for the silver medal after losing to the United States 2–1.

The 1999 Women's World Cup is remembered for the USWNT's famous victory. At the time, however, many were talking about Sun. She had terrorized opponents, scoring a tournament-leading seven goals going into the final.

Sun Wen poses with the Golden Ball trophy she won as the best player of the 1999 Women's World Cup.

The confident Chinese team was favored by many in the final. In the end, both teams locked down defensively. They played to a 0–0 draw. Then the United States won in an iconic shootout. Afterward, however, it was Sun who was awarded the Golden Ball. Many major competitions award a Golden Ball to the best player of the tournament.

In 2001, a new professional league began in the United States. It was called the Women's United Soccer Association (WUSA). Teams selected their players through a **draft**. The Atlanta Beat picked Sun first overall. But Sun is best known for her time with China. She continued playing through the 2003 Women's World Cup. She retired for good in 2006. Over 152 international games, she scored an amazing 106 goals. When FIFA named its female player of the century in 2000, Sun shared the award with American Michelle Akers.

Homare Sawa

In 2011, Japan became the first Asian team to win the Women's World Cup. The star of that team was Homare Sawa. She scored five goals during the tournament. Many expected the United States to win the final. Instead, Japan scored victory in a shootout. Sawa was awarded the Golden Boot (top scorer) and Golden Ball (top player) Awards. She was also named FIFA's 2011 Player of the Year. In 2015 she led Japan back to the Women's World Cup final.

Sun Wen heads the ball during a practice with the Atlanta Beat in 2001.

CHAPTER THREE

MARTA

The odds were against Marta ever becoming a professional soccer player. It was even more unlikely that she would become one of the greatest players in the history of the sport.

Marta Vieira da Silva was born on February 19, 1986, in Dois Riachos, Brazil. Her family did not have much money. They could not afford to buy soccer balls. That didn't stop Marta. She found deflated soccer balls in the street and used those. Sometimes she wadded up grocery bags and kicked those down the street. Marta was determined to play the game.

Growing up poor wasn't the only obstacle she faced. Brazil had banned women's soccer in 1941. The ban was lifted in 1981. However, girls still weren't encouraged to play.

Brazil's Marta is one of the most electrifying players ever to set foot on a soccer field.

There also weren't any girls' teams for Marta to play on. She started playing with a boys' club. Even then her skills stood out. Vasco da Gama is a soccer club in Rio de Janeiro, Brazil. It was starting a women's team. A scout was looking for talented players to join. He soon discovered Marta. She began playing organized games against other women for the first time at age 14.

Vasco's women's team dissolved in 2002. But Marta was just getting started. That same year, at 16, she debuted with the Brazilian national team. Two years later she signed with Umeå IK in Sweden. That made Marta the first Brazilian woman to play professionally in Europe. She helped lead Umeå to the European championship that season.

Marta went on to enjoy a decorated professional career. In 2017 she began playing for the Orlando Pride. That team is in the National Women's Soccer League (NWSL). But she is best known for her international career.

Fierce Formiga

Miraildes Maciel Mota was born in Brazil in 1978. It was illegal for women to play soccer in that country. The ban was lifted in 1981. The woman better known as Formiga made the most of the opportunity. The midfielder played in her first Women's World Cup in 1995. In 2019, she played in her seventh. Two years later she played in her record seventh Olympics. Formiga retired in 2021 after her 234th match for Brazil.

Brazil's Star

Marta played in her first Women's World Cup in 2003 at age 17. She scored three goals in four matches. She added three more goals at the Olympics a year later. That effort helped Brazil win the silver medal.

Marta's shining moment came in the 2007 Women's World Cup.

Marta (right) celebrates a goal with her Brazil teammates.

Brazil faced a powerhouse US team in the semifinals. The Americans hadn't lost in 51 games. Then they faced Marta. She scored two goals in a 4–0 victory. Marta won the Golden Boot with a tournament-high seven goals. And despite Brazil losing the final to Germany, she also won the Golden Ball.

Brazil's best men's players are known for their flair. Marta brought the same style to the women's game. She combined great athleticism with elite skills on the ball. And whatever she did on the field, she made it look good. FIFA first recognized her as its Best Women's Player in 2006. She won the award a record sixth time in 2018.

Marta was honored as FIFA's Best Women's Player for the sixth time in 2018.

Marta played in three more Women's World Cups after 2007. She scored in each of them. That made her the first player, male or female, to score in five World Cups. And her 17 World Cup goals are the most in the history of the sport. In 2021, Marta became the first player to score a goal in five consecutive Olympics, too.

It wasn't easy for Marta and other girls to become soccer players in Brazil. But thanks to Marta, Brazil has become known as a women's soccer country, too.

QUICK FACT

The 2016 Olympics were held in Rio de Janeiro, Brazil. Marta was honored by being one of Brazil's flag bearers at the Opening Ceremony.

Second-Class Soccer?

Brazil has been a men's soccer power for decades. Eventually its women's team became great, too. However, the women did it with much less support. Officials often treated the men's team better. The women were seen as less important. Men's players could also earn a lot more money. Brazil is trying to change that. It took an important step in 2020. Since that year its women's national team players are paid the same as the men.

CHAPTER FOUR

MEGAN RAPINOE

Megan Rapinoe first captured the world's attention for her play with the USWNT. She later used her fame to become a force for change off the field as well.

Megan Anna Rapinoe was born on July 5, 1985, in Redding, California. She and her twin sister had four older siblings. The older Rapinoe kids played soccer. That made the twins want to play too. There were no girls' teams where they grew up. So the twins started out on boys' teams.

Rapinoe proved to be talented enough to earn an athletic **scholarship**. She scored 15 goals and tallied 13 assists as a freshman at the University of Portland. That school isn't known for its sports. But Rapinoe's crafty play as a winger stood out. She helped the Pilots go undefeated

Megan Rapinoe (3) celebrates with teammate Christine Sinclair after scoring a goal for the University of Portland.

and win the national title in her first season. One year later, in 2006, the US national team came calling.

Megan Rapinoe (right) and Abby Wambach teamed up for a huge goal at the 2011 Women's World Cup.

Never Giving Up

Just as Rapinoe's international career was starting,

it appeared to end. Late in 2006 she tore her ACL.

Rapinoe wouldn't play for the USWNT again until 2009. When

she finally made her way back, she made sure she stayed.

Her breakout came at the 2011 Women's World Cup in Germany. Things were not looking good for the US team. It met Brazil in the quarterfinals. The match was tied 1–1 after 90 minutes. Then Brazil took the lead in **extra time**. The Americans appeared on their way to their worst finish ever. And to make matters worse, midway through the second half a US player drew a red card for tripping Marta near the goal. A player who draws a red card is ejected from the match, and her team cannot replace her. That meant the US was playing with only ten players.

The game entered the 122nd minute. The referee would blow the whistle at any time. Rapinoe never gave up hope. She received the ball on the left wing. Then she drilled a long cross toward Brazil's goal. The ball sailed perfectly to teammate Abby Wambach. She headed it in for the tying goal. It marked the latest goal in Women's World Cup history. The United States then went on to win in a shootout. Rapinoe was one of the successful US shooters.

Rapinoe's performance brought new life to the US team. Few players would even attempt such a difficult play.

Megan Rapinoe kisses the trophy after the USWNT won the 2015 Women's World Cup.

And Rapinoe executed it perfectly. That combination of traits helped her become one of the world's most dangerous offensive players.

Although the Americans fell to Japan in the Women's World Cup final, a new era was beginning. Rapinoe was at the center of it. She scored three goals in the 2012 London Olympics. That helped the USWNT successfully defend its gold medal. Three years later, Rapinoe starred in her second Women's World Cup. The Americans overpowered their opponents. Three minutes into the final, Rapinoe assisted on Carli Lloyd's goal. The United States cruised to a 5–2 win. It was their first since the team's landmark 1999 championship.

Equal Play, Equal Pay

Women are often paid less than men across sports. Soccer is no exception. In 2018, the men's World Cup offered $400 million in prize money. One year later just $30 million was awarded in the women's tournament.

And yet Rapinoe's best tournament was still to come. The 2019 Women's World Cup was in France. Rapinoe teamed with Alex Morgan and Tobin Heath to form a dominant forward line for the US team. They proved to be an unstoppable force. Rapinoe and Morgan each scored six goals, and they combined for five assists. The last of Rapinoe's goals came in the final. It opened the scoring in a 2–0 win over the Netherlands. Afterward, Rapinoe was awarded the Golden Ball.

Athlete Activist

By the 2019 Women's World Cup, Rapinoe also had become known for her social **activism**. In 2016, the pro football quarterback Colin Kaepernick began protesting racial inequality by kneeling during the national anthem. The move was controversial. Many believe it resulted in his career being cut short. Wanting to show her support, Rapinoe began kneeling too. That made her the first white athlete to kneel. As with Kaepernick, the backlash was swift. Some people felt she was being disrespectful to the flag. But Rapinoe has never shied away from speaking her mind.

Megan Rapinoe poses with her trophies after the 2019 Women's World Cup final.

Over the years Rapinoe has become a vocal leader on other issues as well. She has voiced support for Black Lives Matter. She is also a leader in the USWNT's efforts to earn equal pay. Her activism has turned some people away. To many others, however, it has made her an even bigger star.

CHAPTER FIVE

CRYSTAL DUNN

Crystal Dunn has won at every level in her soccer career. She has dozens of individual and team awards. And she's done it all while playing multiple positions.

Crystal Alyssia Dunn was born on July 3, 1992, in Rockville Centre, New York. She played soccer from a young age. But early on, she noticed she was often the only Black girl on the field. That made her wonder if she belonged in the sport.

Dunn quickly proved that she more than belonged. She became a superstar for her high school team. Then she became a top college player at the University of North Carolina. In 2012, she led the Tar Heels to a national title. She also won the MAC Hermann Trophy as the best player in college soccer.

Crystal Dunn (19) of North Carolina fights for position with Stanford's Mariah Nogueira during a 2012 match.

At North Carolina, Dunn played as an attacking midfielder. The US team called her in to play at the 2012 Under-20

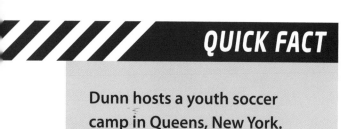

QUICK FACT

Dunn hosts a youth soccer camp in Queens, New York.

Women's World Cup. There she started every game as a right back. Her effort helped the United States defeat Germany for the championship.

Going Pro

There was no doubt that Dunn had a bright future. The question was at which position. In 2014, she entered the NWSL draft. The Washington Spirit picked her first overall. There she played as a forward. And once again she thrived.

Briana Scurry

Briana Scurry made history as the first Black woman and first female goalkeeper to be inducted into the National Soccer Hall of Fame. She saved the day during the US team's win over China in the 1999 Women's World Cup. During that game, Scurry dived to her left to block a shot from China's Liu Ying. That led to Brandi Chastain's game-winning penalty kick.

Crystal Dunn (right) worked on her defense to become one of the USWNT's most dependable players.

But when it was time for the United States to name a team for the 2015 Women's World Cup, Dunn missed out. She was the final player cut.

At first she felt embarrassed. Then she went to work. Dunn scored an NWSL-high 15 goals in 2015. At 23, she became the youngest Most Valuable Player (MVP) in league history. In 2016, she made the US Olympic team. Two years later, she led her new NWSL team, the North Carolina Courage, to the league championship.

At the time, Dunn was best known for her offensive skills. But the US team was loaded with talented goal-scorers. To make an impact, Dunn knew she'd have to again show her **versatility**. And when coach Jill Ellis asked her to play as a left back in the 2019 Women's World Cup, Dunn was ready.

Switching positions required great discipline. Instead of attacking the opposing goal, she had to stop attacks. She studied lots of video to prepare. Using her speed and **endurance**, she was able to stick with the other team's top attackers. With her well-timed **tackles**, she did just that. And at times she even got to join in on the attack. Over seven games, the Americans gave up just three goals. Dunn started in six of those games. Though Dunn didn't get as much attention as some of the goal-scorers, many said she was

Crystal Dunn is honored for playing her 100th match with the USWNT.

one of the team's best players. Most importantly, Dunn's effort helped the United States win another Women's World Cup title.

Few players in the world have reached Dunn's level at one position, much less two. Dunn nearly lost hope when she didn't make the 2015 Women's World Cup as a forward. Instead, she showed that with hard work, she could be just as valuable as a defender, too.

Soccer for All

Dunn is a member of the Black Women's Player Collective. This organization supports Black players. It seeks more representation on US soccer teams. Dunn's goal is to be her true self. She encourages other Black women to feel comfortable in the mostly white world of soccer. She also wants coaches and other players to realize that their words have meaning. They should judge people by their playing skills and not the color of their skin.

The Women's World Cup has become one of the biggest sporting events in the world.

Women have had to fight for equality on the soccer field since the earliest days of the sport. Now, thanks to the hard work and skills of its talented players, women's soccer leagues and tournaments are followed by fans throughout the world.

GLOSSARY

activism
supporting action and discussion for resolving an issue

draft
the process of selecting players for a team

endurance
the ability to keep going for long periods of time

extra time
two 15-minute periods added to a soccer game to break a tie

federal
having to do with the national government

scholarship
money given to a student to attend a school or program

shootout
a tiebreaker used after extra time with each team taking turns trying to score on penalty kicks

tackles
attempts by a defender to take the ball from an opponent

versatility
the ability to change easily

FOR MORE INFORMATION

Books

Jökulsson, Illugi. *Women's World Cup, 2019*. New York, NY: Abbeville Press Publishers, 2019.

McKinney, Donna B. *Women in Soccer*. Lake Elmo, MN: Focus Readers, 2020.

Peters, Stephanie True. *On the Field with…Megan Rapinoe, Alex Morgan, Carli Lloyd, and Mallory Pugh*. New York, NY: Little, Brown and Company, 2020.

Websites

The Equalizer
(equalizersoccer.com)

Read all the big news from the world of women's soccer.

FIFA Women's World Cup
(fifa.com/tournaments/womens/womensworldcup)

Get the latest updates and learn about the history of the Women's World Cup.

UEFA Women's Champions League
(uefa.com/womenschampionsleague)

The top women's clubs in Europe battle to see who's No. 1.

INDEX

ABOUT THE AUTHOR

Joanne Mattern is the author of many books for young readers. Her favorite topics include sports, biographies, science, and history. She loves sharing information with her readers and helping them discover new things. Mattern lives in New York State with her family.